Fire Your Boss!

Fire Your Boss!

The 19 Secrets of Entrepreneurial SUCCESS

Cheryl Thompson

Clarion Marketing Group, Inc.
Lee's Summit, Missouri

Fire
Your Boss

Cheryl Thompson
PO Box 1032
Lee's Summit, MO 64063
www.EncouragementToGo.com
fax 816-537-0729

Published by
Clarion Marketing Group, Inc.

Cover design and typesetting by Ad Graphics, Inc., Tulsa, OK

Printed in the incredible United States of America

ISBN#: 1-931317-00-3

Acknowledgments

This is my favorite part…where I get to thank the incredible people in my life.

My husband, Dennis, who has been my sweetheart and faithful confidante for 26 years, my soul mate and biggest supporter…life with you could never be long enough.

My children, Candice, Kelsey and Travis. You are the loves of my life.

My parents, Mary and Dick Stroud. Thanks Mom and Dad. You know how much your love and support mean to me.

Rhonda Denny, my best friend and "entrepreneurial coach" – you truly launched me and sustain me.

Roger Roberts, my mentor. Thanks for modeling a successful company and encouraging me that the greatest asset I ever needed, I already had.

Ben Weaver, my first boss. His dedication and belief in me were astounding.

Thank you Lord. I have been blessed more than any one woman could be in a lifetime.

All of you not mentioned above, my faithful family, friends and encouragers, (Rudee, Roy, Terri, Sherry, Margo, Deborah, Karen, Janece) you know how much I love you. Thank you!

And to Roxanne Emmerich, you changed my life at the Cavett Institute for Developing Speakers Seminar back in 1999. Thank you for touching my life and giving me the inspiration to do more!

SPECIAL THANKS!

Dee Barwick
Julie & Bill Sherriff, Sherriff & Associates
Kate Sherrill, Indigo & Company

Margo, I am so blessed with you!
What a team!

TABLE OF CONTENTS

" *Nothing happens unless first a dream.* **"**

– Carl Sandburg

Purpose

The purpose of *Fire Your Boss* is to encourage you that self-employment is a viable option. That it's possible. That it's not magic or rocket science. It's not for the overly talented or for people who have great wealth, but for anyone who has a dream, a desire and a plan of action.

The beauty of *Fire Your Boss* is that you don't have to, that is, fire your boss. Take a test run, run your business in the evening or as a hobby to begin with until you can get comfortable with the idea of being the boss.

Getting a business started isn't easy, but I've found it's more difficult to believe you can do it, than to actually do it. *Fire Your Boss* gives you encouragement and a collection of tips that will save you time, money and headaches.

One word of caution. Running a business is NOT for everyone. So before you fire your boss, be sure that it's truly more than something you "think" you should do. Many people believe that running their own business is an inherent part of the American Dream. It isn't. Some of us will work for ourselves, some of us will work for others. And the world needs all of us to function productively.

But if the answer is Yes, then…

Yes, you can! You can become the master of your own destiny. Stick with your plan and with it will come the freedom, the excitement and the rewards of being your own boss.

I know you can do it!

[signature]

YOUR PLAN OF ACTION

Believe!

Get Ready!
Dream Big
Pray
Vision
Action

Invest Learning Time

Successful Entrepreneur to Start   Read   Find a Mentor

Character

Know Yourself – Get Set!
Be Professional
Exude Enthusiasm
Be Accountable
Serve Others
Be a Friend
Never Gossip

The Business

GO!

Action Plan	It's the Package!	Delegate
Debt Free	Bigger Isn't Better	Infrastructure
		Feedback Loop
		Acknowledge Your Fear
		Build Systems

Believe!

> *BELIEF*
> *Your*
> *beginning*
> *and your*
> *anchor*

INTRODUCTION

No limits. Risk. Infinite time and freedom.
Headaches. The ability to make a difference if you choose.
Being the boss...and days when you wish someone else
was the boss. Incredible rewards!

Owning your own business is a great way to create a rewarding life. A life defined by what you determine success is. A life of balance and prosperity. The rewards can outweigh the risks, if you're willing to take the first step.

Going solo can be frightening and exhilarating at the same time. **You'll never know if you can do it until you try!**

Contrary to popular myths about entrepreneurism, working for yourself can provide a life of no limits and incredible balance. It doesn't automatically mean 60-70 hour weeks.

How many solo success qualities do you have?

- A desire to achieve
- Willing to invest time
- A passion for life
- A desire to serve others
- Money is important but not the ultimate goal
- Willing to take risks
- Multi-tasking – can wear many hats
- Hard working but not a workaholic
- Can recognize opportunities

- Love to learn
- Ability to delegate
- Desire to lead
- Find joy in working
- Persevering
- Good resource manager

> *"Do not be anxious for anything, but in everything, by prayer and petition, with thanksgiving, present your requests to God."*
> – Philippians 4:6

PART I.

BELIEVE!

> **"Whether you believe you can or believe you can't, you're right."**
>
> – Henry Ford

SECRET 1

Believe!

B elieve! What's stopping you? Don't let a negative mindset dash your dreams. Believing and dreaming are difficult for most people – beginning in pre-school we're told what to do. We're told to quit daydreaming and that our dreams are foolish and unrealistic. Often, we're told these things by the people who are supposed to love us the most…our parents. We're told that following directions will keep us safe and we begin to let our belief in others take over our belief in ourselves.

Take an inventory of the skills you have. Sometimes it's the un-likely skill, not necessarily a "career" skill, that can help you launch a business.

My business started small. I started doing what I call "miniature" consulting work back in 1990. When my first contract was signed, I didn't even have letterhead or business cards…and I used a contract template that I found in a book, with minor revisions. But when I went in to "sell," they didn't know any of that. I put together a proposal, I dressed to the hilt (even though I was 5 months pregnant and it was hard to "hide") and I used my enthusiasm to fuel my lack of knowledge. I received the contract and went home and danced on the back porch.

You have to believe you can be a successful entrepreneur!

* * * * * * *

Tip: My belief in God is my number one critical element to success. Believe, pray and have faith.

Tip: Think BIG. Big dreams produce big results. Little dreams produce little results.

Tip: Commit to 5 years. Define your vision. Where do you want to be in 5 years? A talented speaker and author named David D'Arcangelo once proclaimed that if you make a five-year commitment TO ANYTHING and persevere, you will be successful.

Tip: Write it down! What gets written, gets done. When you articulate your dreams in writing, you've processed them and made the connections in your brain to bring the concepts you want to life. This does not have to be a formal process – notes in a margin can be good enough.

I believe I can:

_____

_____

_____

_____

_____

_____

_____

_____

_____

_____

_____

Without vision,
you shall perish.

"*1 goal, 10 assists*"

– Adidas television commercial
on USA Women's World Cup
Soccer Team 1999

PERSONAL SUCCESS STORY

Julie Sherriff, Sherriff & Associates
Type of Business: Physician Recruitment

"My ultimate dream was always to own a business. I thought of it often, but believed I did not have the resources or knowledge to own a business. Besides, I was married, had babies and other responsibilities. Then, I went to work for a company on a part-time basis as a clerical assistant. They provided an opportunity for me to learn physician recruitment and I eagerly learned it and ended up loving the field.

*After five years in the division, our company owner had a serious illness and decided to close my division and let everyone go. I asked for an opportunity to buy the business even though there were no employees and I really had no money. What I did have was **knowledge and a great desire**.*

I went to a small business development class at a local college to help me make the decision about purchasing the business. After going over the books, they advised me to walk away. The reason? There was a lot of contingency business (you only get paid when you do a placement of a physician) left on the books but no regular, steady income. In other words, in order to have any income at all, we needed to do a great deal of marketing and selling and fulfillment of old contracts.

Although I recognized the danger in this, I felt I really knew the business and had a passion for it, so I decided to jump in with both feet and go ahead with the purchase.

My landlord gave me a break on office space, I took out a second mortgage on my home, the bank took a chance on me and I was off and running.

Just days after I purchased the business, a new client came to me with several new physician searches and enough retainers to ensure our survival for six months. I truly felt that God was letting me know that I'd made the right choice."

"We act as though comfort and luxury were the chief requirements of life, when all that we need to make us happy is something to be enthusiastic about."

– Charles Kingsley

SECRET 2

Exude enthusiasm!

E nthusiasm is catching. It's the best sales quality you'll ever have. People are accustomed to hearing grumbling and whining, so when they meet someone who's enthusiastic about where they're going or what they're doing, they stop to listen. Get excited about what you do.

Your efforts will pay off. And wouldn't it be great if people referred to you as that "enthusiastic guy who owns the bike shop" or there goes that "perky" woman again!

* * * * * * *

Tip: Smile. They're free!

Tip: Have a firm handshake. As a businessperson, I judge a person's character and capability on the firmness of their handshake. Practice if you have to…and women, your handshake can and should be as firm as a man's.

Tip: Keep your personal challenges to yourself. Don't share negative personal information that has nothing to do with the business at hand. If your dog chewed up the business proposal and your child had to stay home sick, work around it. The client doesn't need to know this.

Tip: Strive to be the "host" of any meeting or get together. Make it your goal to make others feel at ease. Most people are as nervous as you are and will welcome your efforts to be friendly.

> ❝*He is well paid that is well satisfied.*❞
>
> – William Shakespeare

SECRET 3

You are your most important asset!

M ost adults believe that the most important component in starting a business is money. You don't have to be wealthy to start a business. The best advice I ever received from one of my mentors was that I was my own best asset. Capital (via money) was important, but the key ingredients to my success were going to be my skills and my attitude, not my bank balance.

You have to be committed to make an income from day one and manage your expenses wisely.

* * * * * * *

Tip: Start small. Focus on one project at a time and don't worry about having a fancy office or any "extras."

Tip: Invest in the essentials only. Phone, fax, computer, software, nice letterhead – anything that helps you build a great image.

Tip: Don't get so caught up in all the details that you let opportunity pass you by. Everything has an opportunity cost. Don't be penny wise and pound foolish.

Tip: Never take out a loan you don't need and don't bet the farm…you'll end up losing it.

PART II.

INVEST LEARNING TIME

> **"There are three ingredients to the good life; learning, earning and yearning."**
>
> – Christopher Morley

SECRET 4

Invest learning time!

Spend time with other successful entrepreneurs.

In getting started, I spent two sporadic years with a successful woman entrepreneur who owned her own graphic design and printing business. By making the investment of time, we built a strong personal and business relationship.

I gave much of my time for free, being her "idea person," and in return, she showed me the inner workings of her business. My investment in time with her has more than a hundredfold returned to me. And most importantly, I have a great friend in the business.

It was amazing to watch her. She'd get her daughter off to school, go get a bagel and a coke, come back and make sales calls, put the finishing touches on a project, head to the gym and to lunch, back to work for a couple more hours and call it a day.

She wasn't making six figures but she was making a comfortable living and the best part, she wasn't KILLING herself doing it, stressing out and battling a bureaucracy.

* * * * * * *

Tip: Be willing to do anything (as long as it's legal and moral). Run errands. Answer phones. Get the experience you need by volunteering. Invest your time with successful entrepreneurs. It will pay off.

Tip: Schedule time on a monthly basis with a successful entrepreneur. The people I would like to spend time with in the next month are:

Name	Business	Phone #	E-mail	Why this person?
1.				
2.				
3.				
4.				
5.				
6.				
7.				

SECRET 5

Read!

B roaden your world with a book. Your resources as a small business owner are limitless with the help of reading materials. Look for information in books and on the web. It's easy to become knowledgeable fairly quickly on a subject you know absolutely nothing about.

* * * * * * *

Tip: Develop a reading schedule (see the list of recommended reading at the end of this book). Try to read business development books and mix in some fiction for fun and pleasure. Take notes.

Tip: Buy a subscription to a magazine specific to your industry. It will always have up-to-date tips, ideas and profiles of people you may want to emulate.

Tip: Read/research daily. Strive to read for a minimum of 15 minutes per day – it's a start and at the end of one year – **you'll have spent over 91 hours reading**! Awesome.

PART III.

BUILD A SYSTEMATIC INFRASTRUCTURE

> **"An ounce of action is worth a ton of theory."**
>
> – Friedrich Engels

SECRET 6

Build a great infrastructure!

S ystems and procedures. While they sound confining, they are the true freedom and power of your business. Put together great systems early on in your business and you can grow, grow, grow.

Automation can free you to focus on the things you do best. Automate everything you can. Create a system and a procedure for virtually everything. A successful orthodontist I know even has a procedure for how to fold the clean towels. With over 10 office assistants tackling this same task – no one ever has to question how it's supposed to be done and the patient towels are always ready to be used with patients.

* * * * * * *

Tip: Invest in automation. Quickbooks Pro is an excellent accounting program, easy to use, simple to learn.

Tip: Keep all of your client's information in your computer database. As soon as you get someone's business card, transfer all of the information to your database, then throw those little pieces of paper away – you'll lose them anyway.

Tip: Maintain a meticulous client file. Keep a file on all of the details of a project so you know the suppliers you used and the systems you employed to complete that project. Starting from scratch is a waste of time.

Tip: Implement a project tracking system. Bill all expenses to that number and keep track of all hours and expenses associated with that project. How else can you track profitability? Once again, Quickbooks Pro!

*Great things
come in small
packages.*

Big isn't always better!

E ntrepreneurs are challenged to grow, grow, grow. Bigger is not always better – many entrepreneurs have found out the hard way (through bankruptcy court) that more employees and bigger buildings create more overhead and more stress. Figure out what a good balance is for you and set your goals accordingly.

* * * * * * *

Tip: Act as an outsource resource. You don't have to be a big company to service a big company. The Fortune 500 needs small businesses with specific, niche skills to help them accomplish their mission.

Tip: Small companies can "look big." Use a toll free 800#. Make your collateral materials look first rate.

> "*What you can do, or dream you can do, begin it; boldness has genius, power and magic in it.*"
>
> – Johann von Goethe

SECRET 8

Package your product or service!

Make it an "entity" in and of itself.

At our company, we talk about the Clarion "difference" or the Clarion "team." Giving programs, products and projects names makes them real and when you discuss your company with others, you begin to believe it too. Your Monday morning production meeting can become the "Monday Morning Quarterbacks" and the software support service program is just as easily called the "Ultra Plus" program.

Packaging is essential to your success.

- **McDonald's** successfully packaged a simple little bundle of food called the Happy Meal. Millions of children everywhere beg their Moms and Dads to buy this package everyday. The clincher for the Happy Meal – a cute little toy in a kiddie size box that costs a little and brings volumes of business to McDonald's.

- **Zig Ziglar** packages himself as a speaking success.

- **Billy Graham** is known as a modern day prophet.

What will your business be known for?

* * * * * * *

Tip: Name the project and the product. Businesses buy products. Don't just outline the details of a product or service. Name it.

Tip: Once you package a product or service, sell it to other similar organizations. You'll save time and money not having to start from scratch. Duplication is the key to exponential success. Make it once, sell it a million times!

> **"Unless you're in the banking business, don't be the bank."**
>
> – Richard O. Stroud

SECRET 9

Don't be the bank!

You're not in the finance business (unless you're a finance company) so don't feel bad about asking what is due you. Keep your invoices and billing current. **NEVER** be behind in billing. When your invoices are due from your clients – send a statement. If they're past due, call. This isn't the time to be bashful.

One of my favorite designers uses the **"Friendly FAX"** technique...whenever an invoice is even a few days late, he faxes a copy of the invoice over to his client with a friendly reminder. Works every time.

One of my first consulting jobs included a stint with a Women's Rehabilitation Clinic that had developed its own educational product for children. We worked on the project for 10 months (stupid us!) without seeing a single cent of payment. Our client kept insisting that she was on the brink of success and that we would be paid in full for our work as soon as she "received her next round of financing." Another 10 months went by and my partner and I had spent a great deal of our time learning about bankruptcy – which was what our client had filed and left us as 'unsecured creditors.' That was the year I received my **"school of hard knocks"** MBA in finance.

* * * * * * *

Tip: Always work from a contract. If you're offering a professional service – expect 50% up front.

Tip: Don't apologize for your fees – ever.

Tip: Don't undersell yourself. People often expect good quality to be more expensive.

Tip: Don't oversell yourself. Do the research to know what the market will bear and decide where you want to establish yourself.

> **"Obstacles are those frightful things you see when you take your eyes off the goal."**

– Hannah More

SECRET 10

Feedback to improve!

Always be a work in progress.

A work in progress can take decades. True success usually doesn't happen overnight. Never be finished with anything. Strive to do more, to learn more, and to be more. Critique finished projects and determine how you could have improved them.

The feedback loop you create in your own company will continue to follow the theme of improvement. There is no evaluation like self-evaluation. Be critical in a very constructive way. That way you know what to replicate and what to toss. Ponder the mistakes or weaknesses but don't let them freeze your progress. Opportunities usually come our direction at exactly the right time – and negative situations are usually learning experiences that will help build a better future.

Most "overnight" successes actually took decades. The old Chinese proverb tells us that when the student is ready, the teacher appears.

* * * * * * *

Tip: Commit to being a lifelong learner.

Tip: Continue your education. Take community college courses or go to workshops sponsored by your local Chamber of Commerce.

Tip: Travel. Getting out of your comfort zone can unleash creativity.

Tip: Too much information can prove detrimental if it keeps you from taking action. Avoid information overload! Classify and organize what you know and what you need to know. This will provide you with a laser focus on what you're working on at the time.

Implement the KWHDL Chart in your company

For this project:

K	What do I know? _____
	_____
	_____
W	What do I need to know? _____
	_____
	_____
H	How will I find out? _____
	_____
	_____
D	What will I do?_____
	_____
	_____
L	What did I learn? _____
	_____
	_____

PART IV.

CHARACTER —
YOURS!

"You get the best out of others when you give the best of yourself."

– Harry Firestone

SECRET 11

Be professional!

Having a small office or a home office (SOHO) doesn't mean having a second rate office. I've seen home businesses that were world class organizations and "large" companies who looked like a big elephant – slow and plodding.

Voice mail – cell phones – letterhead – business cards – e-mail are all readily affordable items in the information age of the 21st century. Make a company like Kinko's your office away from your office.

There's no excuse to be unprofessional.

> Are you worried about having a "home office?" From experience, I've found that if you don't mention your "home" office, no one ever asks. And incredibly, today it's the "in" thing. Ten years ago you didn't exist if you worked at home, now it's a goal for most people in business.

* * * * * * *

Tip: Invest in a separate phone line from the beginning. Business is business. Home is home. Don't mix the two. Clients may like children, but they don't like hearing them in the background or talking over them.

Tip: Project a first-class image. If you want to run a million dollar business (or more), dress like you're the CEO of a million dollar business. Never show up at a client's place of business in "business casual." Business casual is fine if you're the employee, never if you're the supplier. Always look your best. Hair, nails, clothing, hose, shoes, etc.

Tip: Accessorize wisely. A good writing pen, a nice briefcase and a day planner to keep you organized.

"From everyone who has been given much, much will be demanded and from the one who has been entrusted with much, much more will be asked."

– Luke 12:48 NKJ

SECRET 12

Be accountable!

S imple stuff, but powerful. Deliver on your promises. Show up when you say you will. Return your phone calls. Treat people like you want to be treated. Remember the Golden rule.

In an Internet/E-mail world, it is sometimes easy to forget there are people behind the machines. If you make a promise, keep it. And don't overschedule. Being hurried and rushed doesn't make for a successful presentation to your client.

* * * * * * *

Tip: Time management. Being accountable starts with being organized. Get a planner and use it! Block off your personal time, your spiritual time, your work time…and don't forget to schedule in some fun times!

Tip: Strive for balance. Protect your personal and family time as a lioness protects her young – never make your business an all or nothing proposition. Put God and your family first in your schedule and the rest will take care of itself.

"The best time to hold your tongue is the time you feel you must say something or bust."

– Josh Billings

Never, ever gossip!

Gossip is evil. It drags people to a lower level. Limit your association with people who gossip because guess what? The next time you're not in the room, they'll be talking about you.

Our mothers told us when we were little that if "we didn't have something nice to say, don't say anything at all." Still applies.

This lesson is one I learned the hard way – a good friend worked in a corporation who also just happened to be one of my best clients (the corporation that is) and I heard through the grapevine that she was going to lose her job. Thinking that I was protecting my friend, I told her the news. She went straight to the boss and confronted him and guess whose face was red? Mine! My consequence for unnecessary gossip – losing one of my best clients. My friend resigned from the company and I eventually regained the trust of the client but guess what? It was a HUGE learning experience and one I wish I could do over. It included my personal apology to the Vice President for my breach of trust and to this day, my lips are sealed.

* * * * * * *

Tip: When in doubt, don't say it. Ever.

Tip: Edify people with your speech. You lift yourself to a higher level when you lift up someone else.

Tip: Be like Thumper. Thumper from "Bambi" the Disney animated motion picture says, "If you can't say sumthin' nice, don't say nuttin' at all."

PART V.

BUILD RELATIONSHIPS

"*Service to others is the rent you pay for your room here on Earth.*"

– Muhammad Ali

Become a part of volunteer organizations!

Contribute – and plan to make a difference. <u>Expect nothing in return for your time</u>. You'll be surprised how many good things happen when you expect nothing in return. It's the natural law of the universe, you reap what you sow.

* * * * * * *

Tip: Your church needs you. The rewards are heavenly.

Tip: Local schools need you. They are seeking business partnerships to enhance the lives of their students. Teach a class or a club. Sponsor something.

Tip: Community organizations need you. If you're an accountant, volunteer to do the books. If you're an advertising executive or public relations professional, help with marketing the organization. You'll not only be helping the organization, you'll also be honing your skills and making invaluable contacts.

Tip: Other entrepreneurs need you. Host a committee or plan a free seminar at your place of business for other small businesses.

> **"The purpose of life is a life of purpose."**
>
> – Robert Byrne

SECRET 15

Find a mentor!

Develop a relationship with someone who has "been there and done that." This will save you years in the learning curve. Be willing to be open and honest with them. Share your facts, share your fears. And ask them to share theirs. Listen and develop a relationship based on trust and true friendship.

* * * * * * *

Tip: Choose a mentor wisely…someone who's of integrity and character and whose only definition of success is not found in money and power.

Tip: Call your local entrepreneurial foundation – they sometimes have mentoring programs that will facilitate the learning process. The Ewing Kauffman Foundation located in Kansas City, Missouri is dedicated solely to furthering entrepreneurial success.

Tip: Develop a relationship with a successful entrepreneur and strive to learn everything you can about the way they run their business. Most entrepreneurs are flattered to be asked about their businesses and relish remembering the early days, how it was getting started.

"Watch the purse strings religiously and don't turn over your financials to anyone. Guard your assets — no one has worked harder to build them."

– Julie Sherriff

SECRET 16

Be your customer's friend!

Goes against all the rules doesn't it? Keeping your "professional" distance is a good thing, isn't it? Nope. The good ol' boys network is really the good ol' friends network. People do business with friends – referrals come from friends, and people continue to do business with people they like.

Get to know your clients… know their children's names and hobbies, what they do on Saturday and where they go to church. Find out what their favorite lunch spot is and what kind of car they drive. Send birthday cards. Be corny. Be hokie. Clients love it.

One of my best clients drives a Mustang, is single, has one small child and loves to race stock cars. We have lunch and while we talk business, we mostly talk about life.

It's easy to do business with people when they know you truly care about them. Encourage your clients and be enthusiastic. (There's that word again!)

* * * * * * *

Tip: Write it down in your client file. Jot down notes about the client when you leave a meeting. Make it your goal to leave every meeting with a personal tidbit that is a part of your client's life.

Tip: Be careful. Don't reveal too much personal information about yourself – especially any problems you might be experiencing.

Tip: Make everyday a holiday. Send cards for non-occasions. Sign them and hand write a personal message...Great job! Love working with you! Thanks for being a part of our team! The time you spend will repay you many times.

PART VI.

BALANCE

> *"The best kind of knowledge exists in knowing how to manage the right resources."*

– Cheryl Thompson

SECRET 17

Delegate!

Don't do things you don't know how to,
or it'll cost you.

Don't spend time doing the things someone else can do for you. Learn to delegate your tasks and do the things that will impact your company the most significantly. If you're a consulting engineer and you need to do payroll for your staff, hire an accountant or a payroll company. You'll never miss your tax filings, payroll deductions, state and local tax rates.

Older children can provide a great source of inexpensive labor – use your own kids, use students or call your local college and set up an internship program. Interns are usually brimming with enthusiasm and breathe new life into a company…they get "real world" experience and you get an energetic, grateful employee, and possibly a great contact for the future!

Retirees are another great labor source. They're usually dedicated, committed and don't necessarily need or want a full time job.

* * * * * * *

Tip: Hire smart. Hire the professionals you need to help you on an outsource basis – never put someone on the payroll that you can outsource for the same service.

Tip: Save time doing something right the first time rather than redoing shoddy work.

Tip: Leverage and balance your time. You can't grow if you spend time doing everything yourself. Figure out what you earn per hour and if having it done by someone else is cheaper than the income you could earn, hire it out!

"*Just Do It*"

– Nike slogan

SECRET 18

Acknowledge your fear!

The fear can "fuel" your energy.

I spent my first six years in business being nervous. Was it going to succeed? The clients were here today but could be gone tomorrow. I woke up every morning with a knot in the pit of my stomach.

To this day, I am still fearful to a certain degree. One of my wise mentors recently explained to me that if we entirely lose the fear, we lose the edge. This calmed me and let me know that fear isn't necessarily a bad thing, unless it encompasses us. Fear equals challenge.

* * * * * * *

Tip: Work with your fear. Figure out what it is that you're afraid of and then take steps toward conquering it.

Tip: Nothing attempted is nothing accomplished. Write it down. What gets written, gets done.

Tip: Get going – action cures fear. Doing something is usually better than doing nothing. Don't lose yourself in "analysis paralysis."

Tip: Have faith. Faith is believing in things not yet seen.

PART VII.

Go!

> **"The journey of a thousand miles begins with a single step."**
>
> – Confucius

SECRET 19

Get moving!

B aby steps are fine, but take the first step.

There's no better time than today to start working for yourself. You can start small. You don't have to quit your day job until you get some momentum rolling, and I wouldn't advise betting the farm to hit the big time.

Slow and steady growth is fine and from my experience…the companies who take growth slow and steady end up as some of the most successful ventures. Fast growth companies sometimes burn out and burn people.

* * * * * * *

Tip: Write down your action plan. Include dates, times, budgets, goals, action steps, timelines, costs anticipated, people to use as resources, and any other miscellaneous "stuff." Get specific! Know what it is you want to do, who you want to do it for, who can help you do it and then get to it. It may take many times "organizing" the plan before you get it right.

Tip: Set goals. When you don't have the business rolling, setting goals may seem funny, like taking a shot in the dark. Many times that's the best shot you've got.

Tip: Get busy. Busy people get things done. Don't do busywork – get busy about your business. Make things happen. Get on the phone. Get out in the world.

"Envision the life you want. Then go out and work like mad to get it. Dreams do come true. And it's not magic. Just some inspiration, perspiration and prayer, all mixed together."

– Cheryl Thompson

CONCLUSION

A **re you clinging to the net?**

No, we're not talking about the Internet.

Imagine a safety net. Visualize the safety net that you believe brings safety and security to your life. The net that delivers the paycheck every two weeks. The one that provides health insurance.

Will it catch you when you fall? Possibly. But in the new millennium, we are each responsible for creating our own net. Employers no longer hire for a lifetime and very few of us will receive retirement parties or a gold watch from one organization. We'll work for 5 or 10 different companies in one lifetime.

The "company" safety net doesn't exist. <u>It's only in your mind.</u> The net that you believe is keeping you safe can sometimes put a lock on your heart and on your dreams. The net shuts down opportunities and squelches your vision.

My advice…let go! Let your passion fuel you. Only when you determine to let go of the net can you really fly.

I hope you soar!

[signature]

RECOMMENDED READING

These books can change your life and are highly recommended by Cheryl Thompson, author of *Fire Your Boss*.

The Magic of Thinking Big
David J. Schwartz, Ph.D.
Simon & Schuster

Living the Simple Life
Elaine St. James
Hyperion

The Bible (NIV)
God

Getting Business to Come to You
Paul and Sarah Edwards & Laura Clampitt Douglas
G.P. Putnam's Sons

Rich Dad Poor Dad
Robert T. Kiyosaki
With Sharon Lechter, CPA

Tuesdays with Morrie
Mitch Albom
Doubleday

The Millionaire Next Door
Thomas J. Stanley, Ph.D.
William D. Danko, Ph.D.

Sense of Purpose/Self Integrity/Achieving Balance
Videotape Series and Workbooks
FranklinCovey

ABOUT THE AUTHOR

Cheryl Thompson

Cheryl Thompson, president of the Clarion Marketing Group is an energizing woman entrepreneur with a mind for business and a heart for people. She is a "people" expert who spends her days running an accomplished marketing and advertising firm for Fortune 500 clients. Confined by the limits and bureaucracy that accompany "corporate life" – Thompson founded the Clarion Marketing Group in 1993 as a way to give her the flexibility and freedom to pursue a better balance between work and family.

Cheryl goes beyond the "theories" and gets to the "heart" of making things happen. Her energetic spirit and zest for life make her a sought after speaker, trainer, and business consultant.

Thompson is a 1983 business school graduate of the University of Missouri Columbia, wife to her high school sweetheart, a mom of three, and author of several books including *What A Difference A Dream Makes*, *Success is in YOU!* and *Go for the Goal!*.

Cheryl's mission: To encourage...to motivate...to inspire individuals to be their very best.

Visit her on the web at
www.EncouragementToGo.com or
www.ClarionMarketingGroup.com

LOOKING FOR AN ENTHUSIASTIC SPEAKER?

Cheryl Thompson

Encouragement to GO™!

Cheryl Thompson, author of **Fire Your Boss**, would love to speak to your entrepreneurial group, association or Chamber organization.

> *"Enthusiasm required! It's one of the primary character traits you can't afford to live without!"*
> – Cheryl Thompson

Encouragement to GO™! Cheryl Thompson's speaking and publishing business allows her to energize your group with high energy inspiration and an enthusiastic style that makes learning fun. Program lengths vary.

Program topics include:

- What a Difference a Dream Makes
- Reinspired! Not Retired.™ (age groups 45-65)
- Debt-Free & Prosperous Living
- Exclamation Living: How to Create a WOW! Way of Life
- The Midas Touch: The Golden Rules of Customer Service
- Marketing on a Shoestring
- Fire Your Boss!
- Voyages: A Spiritual Journey Toward Renewal

Thompson spends her days creating programs that give people courage, inspiration and the motivation to go out and create a successful life for themselves. Get ***Encouragement to GO™!*** It will make a difference in your life.

Contact us at:
www.EncouragementToGo.com
www.ClarionMarketingGroup.com

Cheryl Thompson
Encouragement to GO™!
Clarion Marketing Group, Inc.
PO Box 1032
Lee's Summit, MO 64063
Toll free 888-353-4668

ORDER FORM

Book	Each	Quantity	Amount
Fire Your Boss *Tips and motivation for entrepreneurial success*	$11.95		
What a Difference a Dream Makes *Full color 48 page motivational workbook* *to help guide you in reaching your dreams*	$ 9.95		
Go for the Goal! *Key elements of goal setting and why* *it's critical to your success*	$ 9.95		
Success is in YOU! *Learn why you're destined for personal success* *and the steps you need to take to get there*	$ 8.95		
How to Grow a Dream *How to plant and grow the dream for your life*	$ 4.95		

All prices U.S. Dollars	**Sub Total**	
Sales Tax (Add 7.475% for MO resident)		
Shipping & Handling (Add $3 USA per book)		
TOTAL		

Name _____   Date _____

Company _____   Phone _____

Street Address _____

City _____   State _____   Zip _____

E-mail _____

❑ VISA   ❑ Master Card   ❑ Check/Money Order *(payable to Clarion Marketing Group)*

Card # _____

Exp Date _____   Signature _____

Phone: 888-353-4668 • FAX: (816) 537-0729
Mail: Clarion Marketing Group • PO Box 1032 • Lee's Summit, MO 64063
Online: www.encouragementtogo.com